Depression-
Era
Wisdom

Publications International, Ltd.

Mary Wynn Ryan is a professional writer, editor, and consultant who has written user-friendly how-to books, brochures, and articles on a wide range of practical subjects, including household hints, do-it-yourself projects, improving family communication, couponing, choosing contractors for home improvements, business management, and more. She focuses on helping readers get better results more quickly and for less money and strongly believes that the tactics and strategies her parents and other people used to get through the Great Depression are worth their weight in gold to consumers today.

Front Cover Illustration: Photodisc

Back Cover Illustration: PIL Collection

Interior Illustrations: PIL Collection, Shutterstock

Contents

INTRODUCTION

Everything Old Is New Again

*T*here's no getting around it: Times are tough. But the strategies for surviving and thriving in today's economic downturn are right at our fingertips. Scores of the daily lifestyle strategies that folks used to get by during the Depression of the 1930s are still applicable today. Now, as then, pluck is easier to come by than luck, and making the best of what we have is an art form. That's where *Depression-Era Wisdom* comes in.

With this recession comes an old-fashioned realization: Quality of life doesn't depend just on what we can afford to consume. Home remedies, cooking, gardening, and other practical crafts are getting a second look, as are simple, economical ways to have fun and be of mutual support. Inside these pages, you'll find a wealth of clever, common-sense tips that can jump-start your own money-saving ideas.

One thing our Depression-era parents would have loved: Our unprecedented access to millions of bargains available any time of the day or night via the Internet. Instead of wearing

"That man is the richest, whose pleasures are the cheapest."
—HENRY DAVID THOREAU

out shoe leather and burning gas, you can let your fingers stroll the keyboard and comparison shop to your heart's content to find the best deals. Equally important, the Internet lets you shop for income opportunities—jobs and places to sell your unwanted belongings—just as easily. Learn how to use this powerful new tool to achieve an old-time goal: Make some money and save even more.

Being thrifty has extra benefits in these modern times. "Reduce, reuse, recycle" was a Depression-era philosophy long before there was an environmental movement. Only back then, the call was to "use it up, wear it out, make it do, or do without." We'll share hundreds of ways you can waste less and take it easy on your wallet—and the planet. Enjoy these tips, add to them, and remember: This time-tested wisdom can help make your money go further day to day, but the real wealth lies within.

CHAPTER 1

Shopping Strategies

*T*oday, as in the Depression era, you have to shop hard to find what you need at a price you're willing to pay. Our shopping options may be more plentiful than they were in the 1930s, but it's still *caveat emptor:* "Let the buyer beware." Different stores have different strengths, and knowing what to buy where makes it easier to score deals.

In the old days, cash was king, but now—especially when it comes to online and big-ticket purchases—it's wise to pay with a credit card. Using debit cards and cash may keep you from overspending, but these payment methods don't offer much recourse if you're unsatisfied with your purchase. On the other hand, credit card companies will work directly with the vendor to help you dispute payment. Just shop thriftily for cards and use only those that have no annual fees and low interest rates. Of course, the interest rates won't matter much if you make sure never to charge more than you can pay off each month!

What to Buy (or Sell) and Where

Before you spend a dollar, do what your parents did: Shop your closet (and your cupboards, garage, etc.) to be sure what you need isn't already there. Can you adapt something you already have to your purpose? If not, consider these options.

The Classics

Barter

Barter, the most ancient form of business, is popular again. If you can sew, prepare taxes, bake, write résumés or ads, draft a will, repair plumbing, baby-sit, hang wallpaper, or do anything else of value, you can trade your skills for those you don't have. Some barter clubs let you bank credits to be used with other club members. Check online to find something that will work for you.

Specialty Shops

Specialty shops have less inventory breadth but more depth than other stores, and their higher prices are balanced by great seasonal sale bargains and helpful staff. Ask the store

Then Versus Now

In 1930, the average yearly household income (with mostly one income per family) was $1,970; by 1939 it was $1,730, roughly $15,000 in today's dollars. With an average income of less than $2,000 a year, careful budgeting was essential—especially when there were no credit cards, only layaway plans for big purchases!

when they will take final markdowns; that's when you'll save the most. And if having shops near your home is important to you, always shop locally before you go to the mall.

Department Stores

Department stores began popping up in the mid-1800s and hit their stride just before the Depression. They tend to offer a much wider selection of clothing styles and prices, with quality levels comparable to better specialty shops. Look for seasonal deals on store Web sites or in the newspaper. You may also find department staff who will take a real interest in helping you.

Discount and General Merchandise Chain Stores

An outgrowth of the old-time general store, discount stores were called "dime stores" or "five-and-ten-cent-stores" during the Depression era. While most of the originals are gone, today's version lives on in discount mass merchants and, increasingly, in large chain drugstores and dollar stores. You'll find that prices are lower than in department stores, but the quality may be lower, too, so buy items you'll use only for a season or two.

Savvy Savings

Before you spend the money on a membership to a warehouse club, ask for a one-day free pass to shop and compare prices. Also check to see whether you are eligible for a free or discounted membership through your work or some other organization.

*"Economy is a strange thing: It means
buying the big size in a box of cereal
and the small size in a car."*
—ANONYMOUS

Consignment Shops

Consignment shops accept only better-quality, recent goods
in like-new condition. You can find some incredible bargains
on gently used designer and top-quality apparel, fine jewelry,
fine china, and furniture. The selection will be limited, but
prices will be reasonable. Some of the best buys in consignment shops are clothes for formal occasions.

If you're selling, call ahead to be sure the consignment shop
takes your kind of goods and check back to see if your items
have sold. Be aware that the store will keep up to half of the
resale price.

Thrift Shops and Bazaars

Churches, hospitals, and charitable groups run permanent
thrift shops and short-term bazaars where goods are donated
and proceeds benefit charity. Shop here for washable clothing,
charming china, glassware and flatware, and sturdy furniture
you can use as-is for its nostalgic charm or repaint/refinish for
a fresh, current look. (Depression-era furniture made of solid
wood can be refinished if damaged; modern laminate cannot.)

You won't be paid for donations to thrift shops, but you'll
gain a tax receipt for a charitable donation. You'll also reduce
clutter, making your house feel cleaner and roomier.

Hint: For the best merchandise selection, shop thrift stores and consignment shops near upscale neighborhoods. When shopping for used clothing, look for well-made pieces. Rather than shopping for specifics, check out items in your size that go with things you already own.

The New Deals
Outlet/Clearance Stores

Originally created to clear out overstocks, overruns, display goods, samples, and seconds/irregulars, many outlets are still owned by a specific manufacturer. Others are owned by independent retailers who buy last season's product from a variety of quality brand-name makers. Either way, you'll find top-quality and designer goods priced much lower than usual because they're last season's look or because sizes are limited. Make sure you're really getting a deal: Some factory outlet stores also stock current product at their regular retail prices, and some independent "premium" retail outlets supplement their goods with cheaper ones, so inspect before you buy. If you need a formal mother-of-the-bride gown, a fancy French baking dish, or any other durable, high-priced item, look here first to get prestige at a good price.

Online Stores and Auctions

Amazon, eBay, and other online auctions let you reach a greater array of shopper-tunities if you're buying and a much larger audience of potential customers if you're selling.

Check out Overstock.com, Amazon.com, and other multi-category vendors who sell excess merchandise for hundreds of

 other retailers and manufacturers at all price points. It's not an exact science, so if you don't know the vendor's site name, start by typing something like "discount designer shoes," "clearance camping equipment," or whatever else you're seeking into your search engine. Keep in mind that the listings at the top of each page (usually in a tinted area) and in the right-hand column of the page are paid listings similar to ads. Listings that appear against the white background are the sites that your search found "organically"—these naturally have enough in common with your request to appear in the results. The closest matches to your request usually appear on the first page.

Pay close attention to the reputation of the auction site itself and the comments of prior customers about the specific online vendor before you buy anything online, and use Pay-Pal or a credit card—never cash or money order.

If you're selling, take good-quality photos of your item from all angles on a simple white or light-blue background, then write up an accurate, complete description of the item including size, material, brand, and so forth. Organize the auction, and ship the item to your "customer" via UPS or the post office. If you have a lot of items or don't want to take the time, contract with a "trading assistant" who will do the eBay selling for you and take a percentage of the proceeds for their labor.

Tips and Resources
Worth Checking Out

✦ Social Security was created by the federal government during the Depression to prevent seniors from starving. If you are still working, make sure all of your earnings are being credited to you: Once each year, call the Social Security Administration at 1-800-772-1213 and ask to have your free Personal Earning and Benefit Estimate Statement sent to you.

✦ Protect your money from identity theft: When you clean out your personal records and files, shred or tear up financial papers and other sensitive documents and scatter them in several trash cans. Thieves dig through garbage cans looking for financial information such as old checks, credit card receipts, bills, bank statements, preapproved credit card applications, or anything else they can use for fraudulent transactions.

✦ Ask your doctor for free samples of prescription drugs he or she is contemplating prescribing for you.

✦ Coupons can offer good money savings but only if the item is something you buy anyway or something you've wanted to try. Also check to make sure the item's price with a coupon is better than the generic or house brand version's regular price.

✦ For free or low-cost classes and demonstrations, check with your favorite home improvement store, craft and hobby store, fabric and sewing store, kitchen specialty store, or computer store to see what their offerings are.

Voices from the Depression Era

"Shopping at home isn't new with the Internet. Mama could shop without ever leaving the house because in the 1930s almost everything was available from door-to-door salesmen. Just for the distraction, we were always happy to see the salesmen from Fuller Brush, Watkins Vanilla, and *The Saturday Evening Post*. There were also the regulars: the milkman who came every day but was seldom seen, the ice man who came only in the summer and only if you left the card in the window, and the coffee man. There was also a salesman who came with a huge black suitcase and sold anything he could carry, from jewelry to vacuum cleaners. He was not popular with Dad who suspected (with cause) that Mama bought some of those big-ticket items on credit!"

—Evelyn R.

✦ Visits to the library are up 30 percent in this recession as people rediscover the national treasure local libraries have been since before the Depression. Books, movies, games, music, and more are all available for little or no cost, plus you'll find free or low-cost entertainment and educational programming for all ages. The library also offers computers for public use, reference and research materials for job hunters, and access to information on government services and programs. If you're not sure what you want or need, you can't go wrong if you start at your public library.

✦ You can rent movies on DVD, but it's still a thrill—as it was during the Depression—to see a film in a real movie theater. To save, go to a matinee instead of an evening show and pay up to 50 percent less. Some theaters also offer matinee prices all the time to seniors and students, so bring your ID. But don't blow your savings at the concession stand. Having a snack at home before the film is much more economical.

✦ Live entertainment was more common during the Depression, and there's still nothing like it. If professional big-city theater is out of reach, enjoy the local talent of community, college, and high school theater groups. Some are as good as professionals, and they'll appreciate your support. If you live near a resort or vacation area, summer stock theater or music festivals offer great value.

✦ If you're interested in seeing a professional show in a major city, keep in mind that you can often get discounted theater tickets for same-day shows. Check online to find out where to buy discounted tickets. Buy your tickets early in the day, before they sell out. Or, look in the newspaper or online for personal ads from season ticket holders wanting to sell some of their tickets to professional shows, games, and the like.

Senior Discounts and Deals

Some deals for seniors start at age 50 while others don't kick in until age 65, so be sure to ask!

✦ At the bank: Look for no-fee checking accounts, discounted or free safe deposit box rental, and free traveler's checks.

✦ At the golf course: You'll receive discount greens fees at most public and many private golf courses.

✦ At natural attractions: At age 62, apply for a $10 Golden Age Passport: a lifetime pass for free admission for you and anyone in your noncommercial vehicle into any federal park, monument, forest, or recreation area that charges an admittance fee. Write National Park Service, P.O. Box 37127, Washington, DC, 20013.

✦ In retail stores: Plan your weekly shopping around your favorite stores' senior discount days (generally Tuesday or Wednesday).

✦ In restaurants: Have dinner early (usually before 5 P.M.) and enjoy Senior "Early Bird" discounts. (Eating dinner earlier is healthier, too!)

✦ At hotels, with insurance, and more: The American Association of Retired Persons (AARP) is a nonprofit organization open to anyone over the age of 50, retired or not. The nominal annual membership fee also includes your spouse. AARP membership gets you discounts on hotels, motels, car rentals, on some insurance, and much more. Call 202-434-AARP.

What to Buy When

Timing is everything in retail: Well-run stores (whether online or offline) have a set schedule for marking down merchandise; you can save up to 80 percent by waiting a few days, weeks, or months. If where you live doesn't get bitter cold until January, score a top-drawer coat at huge savings right after Christmas. Shop after Easter for perfect spring apparel you'll wear to weddings and graduations in May and June. If your vacation is in August, don't buy that designer bathing suit until July, and shop for exterior house paint in September. Of course, if sales are slow, bargains may appear earlier. Use these listings to start your shopping plans, check the newspaper and free shoppers for big sales, and go online to check when sales are being held at your favorite stores.

Spring: Look for coats, appliances, china, glassware, ski equipment, storm windows, hosiery, luggage, tires, snow tires, lingerie, summer clothes, handbags, housewares, men's clothing, blankets, bathrobes, TV sets.

Summer: Shop for furniture, luggage, lingerie, summer sportswear, building materials, dresses, men's suits, patio furniture, air conditioners, shoes, vacuum cleaners, summer clothing, carpet, linens, gardening tools, sporting goods, new cars, camping equipment, home office/school supplies, clearance bathing suits.

Fall: Get a deal on housewares, cars, hardware, garden supplies, automobiles, car batteries, dishes, mufflers, paint, women's fall clothes, hosiery, lingerie, major appliances, silverware, camping equipment, glassware, blankets, dresses, water heaters, men's shoes.

Winter: Keep an eye out for clearance coats; clearance men's clothes, women's dressy apparel and shoes; dishes; home

"November runs into December, December runs into Christmas, and Christmas runs into money."
—ANONYMOUS

furnishings and decorative accents; holiday decorations and cards; bed linens; towels; and giftware.

Holiday Cheer: Christmas comes but once a year, but you can shop for it all year 'round instead of going for broke the last month of the year. Start at the sales in January when decorations and cards go for 50 percent off. Don't buy things that may be out of date, outgrown, or out of warranty by next Christmas but *do* buy durable, classic home goods like cookware, table linens, hand tools, and long-standing hobby gifts.

Healthy Savings

Health care was a luxury during the Depression—just as it is now—so folks did what they could. Some home remedies worked, others didn't, and a few did real harm. Today, you can stay healthy, solve small medical problems, and minimize the big pain of medical costs with the following tips:

✦ Don't pay extra for brand-name vitamins; read the labels and look for generics with the same contents.

✦ For homemade ice packs without a watery mess, use a package of frozen peas or other vegetables. For a quick, temporary hot-water bottle, pour hot (not boiling) water into an empty plastic soda bottle, screw the top on tightly, and wrap the bottle in a towel.

✦ Avoid unhealthy drug interactions: Before treating your-self with an over-the-counter medication ("natural" or otherwise), always ask your pharmacist if it's safe to use with any other medications you're taking. Also ask about money-saving generic equivalents.

✦ To minimize the high cost of drugs, use the discount mail-order pharmacy from The American Association of Retired Persons (AARP), available to anyone, regardless of age. This full-line drugstore carries prescription medication and over-the-counter items. Their prices are hard to beat, so call for a quote: AARP Pharmacy (1-800-456-2226).

✦ The family doctor who makes house calls is long gone, but today, walk-in medical clinics—some conveniently located in chain drugstores—offer drop-in help relatively quickly. Medical credentials should be prominently displayed in any medical office, so check them with care.

✦ Check with your local health department, your local hos-pital, and neighborhood walk-in clinics for free or low-cost

Then Versus Now

In the 1930s, men's shirts sold for $1.45–$2.50 and slacks for $3.98. A man's sport coat was $19.98. Men's overcoats and women's winter coats were $15 and $16. A practical pair of ladies' oxford shoes went for $2.44, dress shoes for $3.45, and silk stockings for 49 cents. A woman's two-piece suit was $6.98, and the latest dress style was $5.75.

cholesterol screening, flu shots and other immunizations, vision and hearing testing, and blood-pressure testing. Elected bodies often sponsor community health fairs where you can get free screenings.

✦ Hospitals also offer free lectures on various health topics to maintain their nonprofit status under the law. Some even offer free exercise classes and free diet and nutrition counseling. Call or check online for details.

✦ Exercise is the body's own lubricant, making everything function better—even your brain. Check with your local park district, hospitals, churches, and women's clubs for inexpensive exercise classes. You'll meet some new friends, get in better shape, and save money at the same time. If your work schedule doesn't match exercise classes, make your own inexpensive exercise DVD by recording exercise shows on TV so you can work out whenever you find the time. Invite friends on the same schedule to join you for added fun.

✦ If you live near a medical or dental school, see if they offer low-cost or free health and dental services as part of medical and dental students' training. Students are supervised, and you'll get to take advantage of the newest procedures and practices.

✦ Don't be embarrassed to ask your doctor and dentist about fees, especially if you are a new patient. This alerts them to your interest in keeping costs down and encourages them to take a look at prices. Some even provide a small discount to long-standing patients. If you have no or inadequate health insurance, be sure to tell all of your doctors and dentists. They know uninsured people are charged far more than the negotiated prices the insured enjoy and may cut you a break.

Home Insurance Savings

Read the fine print of your insurance policies and talk to your agent each year about discounts you may have already earned by installing smoke alarms, sprinklers, and burglar alarms; upgrading electrical, heating, or plumbing facilities; and adding fences. Discounts may be available for new homes, for retirees, and for claim-free customers.

Comparison-shop your insurance every year and politely ask your existing carrier to match any new, better quotes you receive. (Before you switch, consider your carrier's track record: Cheap insurance that doesn't cover what you need or pay off without a hassle is a false economy you can't afford.) If you have found your carrier dependable, insure your house, cars, and the like with that company and pocket the loyalty discount.

To save big on your homeowner's insurance, consider raising your deductible.

Save, Save, Save

The goal of a frugal lifestyle is not just to make ends meet but to have enough money leftover to save for the future. Here are simple tips from the good old days:

✦ Pay yourself first: Start a savings account and add to it every payday, even if it's just $10 or $25 a month.

✦ When you pay off a car loan or other installment loan, continue to make the "payments" to your savings account.

✦ Save all your loose change in a jar; whenever the jar is full, deposit the coins into savings. Deposit all rebate checks and money saved using coupons into your savings account, too.

✦ If you're one of the lucky ones who still gets a raise, have the additional money go directly to your savings account. Put any bonus checks or overtime pay into your savings account, too.

✦ Jump-start your savings account by having a yard sale and depositing the proceeds.

✦ If you receive an income tax refund, deposit it into savings.

✦ More than ever today, you need an emergency fund: Save enough money to pay all your monthly expenses for at least six months and keep it accessible for an emergency in a regular bank account or in a money market mutual fund.

✦ If you carry credit card debt, pay it off while building your savings account. Emergency savings are vital, but the difference between the interest you're earning on your savings and the interest you're paying on your cards is huge, so you're actually losing money if you don't pay off the cards. Pay off the debt with most of your available funds—put the most money toward the card that charges the highest interest first—but sock away a little in savings, too. As

"Credit is a clever financial trick that enables us to spend what we haven't got."
—ANONYMOUS

soon as you have paid off the card(s), start making payments to your savings account each month.

✦ Once you get the cards paid off, stop using the ones with the highest rates and stick with a few low-interest, no-fee cards. Everyone needs a credit card these days, and if your credit history or job is at all shaky, you don't want to be cut off from credit now! But keep usage of high-interest cards to no more than you can pay off each month.

✦ If a big emergency bill means you can't pay it off within the month, at least pay something on all cards, on time, to avoid monthly penalties and a blighted credit rating. Always pay more than the minimum: If you charge $2,000 and pay only the minimum each month, it can take 30 years to pay off and cost you thousands in interest!

✦ If a low-interest credit card offer seems too good to be true, it probably is. Read the fine print before committing to a card.

✦ Don't take cash advances at ATMs or with checks: You'll be charged interest from the first day. Instead, get cash the old-fashioned way: from your bank account.

✦ Review your credit report yearly: An error on your credit report might cause you to be turned down for a car or home loan.

CHAPTER 2

Healthy, Wealthy, and Wise

*I*t might be hard to imagine in this day and age, but during the Depression, many people had only a few changes of clothing. Items were often sewn at home, and people treasured the finer goods they bought and inherited. Today, of course, a wide array of retail stores, including many online, make it easy to look well dressed on a budget—if you know when and where to shop and how to get the most wearings for your money.

Frugal Meets Fashion

By now, you probably know what shapes flatter your body, what colors flatter your skin tone, what sizes you typically find comfortable, and what your overall style (and lifestyle) is. That's important because most people have stuffed closets, overheated credit cards, and "nothing to wear" because they bought things that don't work for them. Never buy anything that doesn't fit you in *all* of the above areas. Sell off your mistakes in a yard sale, and you'll be money ahead.

To see if a buy is a bargain, calculate your cost-per-wearing. If a trendy T-shirt costs only $15 but it falls apart in the wash after two wearings, that's $7.50 a wearing; if a blazer on sale costs $150 and you can wear it once a week for eight months (32 times), that's $4.68 per wearing.

Spend more on classic, versatile main pieces you'll wear weekly all season and less on trendy items. You can also spend less on items you don't wear often, such as cocktail apparel, but this doesn't mean buying at mass merchants. Instead, shop online at premium/designer outlets or check boutiques for quality gowns at the end of the season. Buy simpler evening garb and dress it up to whatever level you choose with your own costume or real jewelry; simpler styles convey quality.

Add what you want to your wardrobe and prune out what you don't—all for free: Host or attend a clothing swap party. E-mail friends to bring a shopping bag or two full of apparel, shoes, and fashion accessories that don't work for them anymore. (You'll want at least two people of each size; others can shop/bring accessories that fit anyone.) Specify that all pieces have to be clean and gently used or new. No money changes hands; friends just take what they like and leave what they

Then Versus Now

During the Depression, you could buy a woman's winter coat for $28 and a man's overcoat for $18.50. A sweater was just $1, probably because many women still knitted or sewed some clothing at home.

"He who buys what he does not want will soon want what he cannot buy."
—ANONYMOUS

don't. Simple refreshments are served, and items remaining at the end of the night go back to the original owner or to charity.

In the Depression, when most women still sewed, more of us knew quality when we saw it. Today, designer labels are no guarantee of quality, so ignore labels unless you know a brand that suits you and holds up well. Instead, look for quality material and good workmanship.

Cheap goods (as distinguished from better goods on clearance) have a hidden price. They are cut smaller than better goods tagged the same size and have smaller seam allowances so it's hard to alter them. They use cheaper thread and fabrics. Some savvy home sewers make it a habit to reinforce all seams, buttons, and buttonholes when they buy a cheap garment, but there's no solution for an item that fades or falls apart due to cheap fabric and dyes.

To get the most for your money, be sure that:

✦ Pockets lie flat and have reinforced corners

✦ Snaps, buttons, buckles, and other trim items are firmly sewn on, not glued

✦ Buttonholes are reinforced with stitching around the holes

✦ Zippers are sewn in straight, lie flat, and match the garment

✦ Hems are straight, and hem stitches are invisible on the outside of the garment

✦ There are no visible stains or wear marks

✦ Rows of stitching are even—not meandering around—and stitches are small, close, and neat, with no loose or hanging threads

✦ Seams and darts lie flat, with no puckering

✦ Fabric has no uneven weaves or slubs (unless it's natural to the fabric, as in raw silk or silk-look rayon)

✦ Plaids, stripes, and checks match perfectly at the seams, including armhole and crotch cross-seams

Fit is a key indication of quality, so never buy anything that doesn't fit (or that a tailor can't make fit for a reasonable price).

Extend Clothing Life

Don't dry-clean when you can air out: Unless they show visible spots or don't smell fresh, wool suits and other dry-cleanable items can be worn more than once before dry-cleaning. After each wearing, remove any smudges with a soft-bristled brush and hang the garment so that wrinkles smooth out (in the steam from a shower works fastest), then air out. When you do dry-clean, always do both parts of a suit at the same time. Be sure to point out any stains and tell your cleaner what caused them.

Don't dry-clean when you can launder: Dry-clean sport coats, suits, and other structured formal business or business-casual clothing, but to save money, stick to washable fabrics for leisure clothing. If an item's tag says "dry-clean only," that's what you need to do, but if it says "dry-clean," you can safely hand-wash or wash in the machine on the delicate cycle using a gentle Woolite-type cleaner, cold water, and no bleach; then hang, lay flat, or air-dry in the dryer. Unstructured, unlined garments of cotton, linen nylon, ramie, polyester, and even silk and some wools can be washed by hand as long as they are colorfast. To test for colorfastness, blot a white rag dipped in hot water on an inside, unexposed seam of the garment. If the color comes off onto the white rag, you'll have to have the item dry-cleaned.

Pretreat before laundering: To remove "ring around the collar" stains, drizzle a little cheap, plain shampoo (not a shampoo-conditioner) on the stain and let it soak overnight

Voices from the Depression Era

"My father was the U.S. postmaster for the little town we lived in, so he always had a steady income, but there was very little to spare. My mother had died a year before the Depression hit, so I did all of the cooking and cleaning for my father and brothers starting when I was nine, as well as going to school. I didn't have any older sisters so the only clothes I got were from grown-up older aunts and such, and the clothes were mostly dark and scratchy and big on me. I got my first new winter coat that wasn't a hand-me-down when I was 22. My husband bought it for me. I always made sure my daughters had pretty clothes." —Maggie H.

~~~~~~~

*"Money: The mint makes it first, and
it's up to us to make it last."*
—ANONYMOUS

~~~~~~~

before washing. To remove stains caused by berries, tomato sauce, and other colored fruit and vegetables, make sure the fabric is washable, spread the stained area across the sink, and carefully pour boiling water on the stain, then wash. To remove a stain from blood or other protein, immediately rinse in cold water and treat with an enzyme presoak or chlorine bleach (only if the item is white and bleach-safe); then wash in cool water.

To remove a grease spot, sprinkle a heavy coat of plain talcum powder on the stain and let sit overnight to absorb the grease. Use a clean, stiff brush to remove the talc and the spot will usually come with it.

To keep your bathing suit from wearing out in a season or two, always rinse it in cold water after swimming, especially if you've been in a chlorinated pool.

If the Shoe Fits...

"...buy it in every color." Or at least in black, camel, brown, and bone (much more chic and versatile than white) to go with everything. If the price is right and the shoe feels good, it can be a wise investment that saves you money on podiatrist's bills.

Look for seasonal deals but never buy cheap shoes for work or walking around—you won't wear them if they hurt, and they won't hold up either. Well-made, genuine leather shoes, handbags, and other leather goods still say a lot about you to some people today, just as in the old days. Premium outlets are a great place to find high-end, name-brand shoes for men and women at discount prices. Look for classic styles as well as classic colors.

For the best fit, try on shoes late in the day when your feet are swollen. Wear the same type of hose or socks that you plan to wear with the shoes and always try on both shoes of the pair. Walk around for a few minutes to make sure they feel comfortable. If they aren't comfortable in the store, don't buy them; they can't be "broken in." Look at fit more than size; shoes should be wide enough in the front for you to comfortably wiggle your toes. The back of the shoe should be tight enough to grip your heel and not slip when you walk but loose enough not to pinch or rub.

When you buy a new pair of workout or tennis shoes, don't automatically throw away the old ones. Save them to wear around the house and keep the oldest pair of comfortable shoes in the garage for painting, gardening, and other chores. To increase the life of your new workout shoes, wear them only for exercise.

When shoelaces get too frayed to lace, dampen the ends with water and twist them tightly, then dip them into clear nail polish and let dry. Your laces will be like new again. To keep the tips on new shoelaces from breaking off, dip them in clear nail polish and let dry before you wear them.

Beauty on a Budget

When it comes to makeup and beauty products, research repeatedly shows that drugstore brands are just as good as most high-end department store and salon products, so try the economical brands first. Looking great on a budget is easier than it has ever been.

A high price doesn't always indicate a better product. An owner of a famous-name cosmetics company once said, "What we are selling is hope in a bottle." In other words, romancing the merchandise creates a lot of its apparent value. Read beauty aid labels for ingredients: You'll be surprised at how similar some products really are. Don't pay top prices when a lower-cost alternative is available.

Where you shop for health and beauty aids can make a big difference when it comes to price. Picking products up at the grocery store may be convenient, but you'll pay for it. Find a drugstore in your area that offers deep discounts on health and beauty aids. It is worth an extra trip once or twice a month to stock up on toiletries.

Many simple home beauty treatments have been used since before the Depression. Take a look at the sidebar on page 31 to see if these low-cost substitutes work as well for you as the commercial versions do.

Savvy Savings

Before applying nail polish, rub your fingernails with cotton balls dipped in vinegar. This not only cleans your nails thoroughly, it also will help nail polish stay on longer.

Cosmetics on the Cheap

Makeup remover: Try baby oil

Bath oil: Mix baby oil and a little perfume

Dusting powder: Use baby powder or cornstarch

Toothpaste: Mix 1 tablespoon baking soda, $1/2$ teaspoon salt, $1/4$ teaspoon peppermint extract

Mouthwash: Use hydrogen peroxide

Mild astringent: Use witch hazel or hydrogen peroxide

Exfoliater: Mix a teaspoon of sugar with your soap lather

Natural complexion mask: Puree 1 tablespoon instant dry milk, $1/2$ peeled cucumber, and 1 teaspoon of plain yogurt in a blender until smooth. Apply the mixture to your face, avoiding the eye area, and let dry for about 20 minutes. Rinse with cool water and pat skin dry.

Muscle-soothing bath: Add $1/2$ cup baking soda to your bathwater

Soothing facial cleanser: Mix $1/2$ cup of mayonnaise, 1 tablespoon melted butter, and the juice of one lemon. Store the mixture in a glass jar in the fridge. Rinse your face with cold water after cleaning.

Hair deep-conditioner: Crack a fresh egg into olive oil; mix together and massage into your hair. Rinse, then wash as usual.

If you stay in hotels that provide small bottles of shampoo, save and refill the bottles for your next trip instead of buying new travel sizes of your regular products.

To save on haircuts, check with local beauty schools

Savvy Savings

Don't throw away thickened nail polish: Carefully put a few drops of polish remover in the bottle, close tightly, and shake thoroughly.

to see if you can get a free haircut during a class. Either the instructor will cut your hair as a demonstration for the class, or a student will cut it with close supervision—often for less than half the price of a salon cut. Ask about hair coloring, perms, and other services too.

To save money when coloring your hair at home, pick a hair color close to your natural color—just a shade or two lighter or darker. With a close shade, you won't have to touch up the color as often. To cover gray, use root touch-up products between colorings.

When you think your shampoo bottle is empty, fill it ⅓ full with water and shake it. You'll end up with enough product for several more shampoos. To get every last bit of lotion out of a bottle, put it in the microwave for 15 to 20 seconds to get it warm (not hot). Or toss the bottle in your bathwater to warm it up; the warm lotion will then pour right out of the bottle.

Protect blonde hair from turning greenish in chlorine pools: After your swim, just rub a little tomato juice on your hair, let it soak in for about two minutes, and wash as usual.

CHAPTER 3

Penny-Wise Home and Garden Care

Concocting homemade cleaning supplies is nothing new—people have been doing it for ages. As an added bonus, homemade products tend to be more eco-friendly and less expensive than commercial products. You can also save by using the simplest, nonbranded formula of basic cleaners such as ammonia, or by buying concentrated versions of products and adding the required water yourself at home.

Homemade Cleaning Products

Most household cleaning jobs can be handled with baking soda, vinegar, or ammonia, so buy these products in the most economical sizes (usually the largest). Also try some of these easy homemade cleaners you can make from household products and other cleaning supplies. (Some "green" products don't kill germs, so use the right solutions for the right jobs.) Important: Always label any homemade cleaners to indicate their contents and never mix cleaners or reuse bottles without rinsing them thoroughly. For safety's sake and to reduce waste from spills, use a funnel for pouring, and protect your eyes and skin.

✦ **All-purpose cleaner:** Pour 1 tablespoon liquid dish soap into a small spray bottle and add 1 cup clear ammonia.

✦ **Window cleaner:** Pour ½ cup rubbing alcohol, 1 tablespoon ammonia, and 1 pint water into a spray bottle. Use old newspapers or clean rags and socks instead of paper towels for a lint-free shine.

✦ **Furniture polish:** Mix ½ cup vegetable oil with ¼ cup lemon juice and store in a clean plastic or glass bottle. Pour a little on an old cotton rag (old white T-shirts work best), and polish wood furniture until oil is absorbed.

✦ **Wall cleaner:** Mix ¼ cup baking soda or borax, ½ cup white vinegar, and 1 cup ammonia in 1 gallon warm water. Always wash walls from the bottom up, since wash water dripping down the wall can leave permanent streaks.

✦ **Drain cleaner:** To help prevent grease buildup and to keep drains smelling fresh, pour ¼ cup baking soda down the drain, add ½ cup white vinegar, cover drain tightly for a few minutes, and flush with cold water.

Then Versus Now

In 1930, the average new house cost $7,145. By 1939, it was down to $3,800. In 1934, you could buy a five-room stucco house in California with a separate garage for $3,750.

*"When your outgo exceeds your income,
your upkeep is your downfall."*
—ANONYMOUS

✦ **Tough cleaning jobs (air vents, shower stalls, etc.):** Add $\frac{1}{4}$ cup baking soda, $\frac{1}{2}$ cup vinegar, and 1 cup clear ammonia to 1 gallon hot water. Wear rubber gloves and clean in a well-ventilated area.

✦ **Grease and ink remover:** Use rubbing or pure alcohol (91 percent) from the drugstore.

✦ **Laundry presoak and stain remover:** Mix $\frac{1}{2}$ cup ammonia, $\frac{1}{2}$ cup white vinegar, $\frac{1}{4}$ cup baking soda, 2 tablespoons liquid soap, and 2 quarts water.

To remove lime deposits in the bath, try hydrogen peroxide instead of expensive, caustic lime removers. (Hydrogen peroxide also works as a mouthwash and as a pain-free disinfectant for cuts.)

Sponges and reusable disposable cleaning cloths are a haven for bacteria, but you don't have to replace them constantly. Just dip your sponge into clean dishwater and rinse after each use, then prop it up to air-dry fast. You can also wash sponges in the dishwasher. Never ball up a wet cleaning cloth; instead, hang it where it can quickly air-dry.

Before you use a chlorine bleach mildew remover, try rubbing alcohol.

To clean stubborn hard-water rings in the toilet bowl, pour a can of cola into the bowl and let it sit for one hour.

Don't keep replacing plastic shower curtain liners: Just wash in the washing machine with a couple of dirty towels to create a scrubbing effect. For stubborn soap scum, add 1 cup white vinegar to the rinse cycle. Hang the shower curtain immediately and let it drip-dry in the shower.

To keep from wasting scouring powder, cover half of the holes at the top of the container with masking tape.

Skip costly air freshener sprays and plug-ins unless they actually kill germs. (Germ-killing sprays are another matter; some are effective, some not, so check *Consumer Reports* before you buy.) To scent a room, put a few drops of perfume on a cotton ball and wipe it on lightbulbs around the house. When you turn lights on, the heat releases the scent. (To prevent shattering bulbs, never damp-wipe a bulb that's hot.)

Freshen your kitchen garbage disposal by throwing the rind from an orange or other citrus fruit into the grinder.

To remove the smell of cutting onions from your hands, rub hands with a slice of fresh lemon.

> *Savvy Savings*
>
> Don't spend money on white plastic bags to line your small wastebaskets and under-the-sink bathroom trash cans: Use the thin plastic bags your groceries come in instead (just be sure they don't have tears in the bottom).

*"The only food that never goes up
in price is food for thought."*
—ANONYMOUS

Supermarket Savings Strategies

Don't shop at the mini-mart unless you're on the road; it's far too expensive. Instead, plan to shop once or twice a week at the supermarket. Look at the special food section of the newspaper (usually available mid-week) or check for coupons online, and make a loose plan for what you'll be eating based on what you like that's on sale. Always shop with a list of what you'll need for the week, and dedicate a section of your list to replenishing paper towels and other household basics before you run out.

Coupons gained popularity in the 1930s and are still popular today. A recent study by the Association of Coupon Professionals indicated that coupons are used most frequently by educated middle- and upper-middle-class consumers. If you have the time

Then Versus Now

In 1939, you could buy a large loaf of sliced bread or five pounds of spinach for a nickel. You could get 14 oranges for a quarter, sharp Wisconsin cheese for 23 cents a pound, ten pounds of potatoes for 19 cents, chuck roast at 15 cents a pound, spring chickens for 20 cents a pound, and hot dogs for 8 cents a pound. A 25-ounce can of Heinz beans was 13 cents; ketchup was 9 cents a bottle; and bacon was 38 cents a pound.

Online Couponing

If you're a faithful coupon clipper, you'll be thrilled to know that "e-coupons" are easily available anytime via your computer. What's more, the Internet lets you in on a world of group buying discounts you couldn't get on your own. Here are a few examples of the many sites out there today. Check them out!

Groupon.com provides different daily deals on restaurants, sightseeing, shopping, and more in approximately 40 major cities in the United States and in other countries too. Groupon uses group buying power to earn participants significant discounts. A certain number of people need to sign up for the deal for all participants to earn the discount, so if you'd like a certain dining experience, for example, you may want to encourage friends or family to sign up with you.

Tippr.com offers deals similar to Groupon; both sites let you sign up for newsletters that give you special deals in your geographic area. Tippr also advertises "accelerated deals" that get better as more people sign up for a particular deal. The more participants, the bigger the discount for each person.

Also keep in mind that most national and regional brands and many national and regional chain stores offer coupons online as well as in the store.

Spend a little downtime online and search out your favorite coupons and deals. With a little practice, you can save on just about everything you need, and you won't have to contend with all those little scraps of cut-out paper!

to find, clip, and sort them (or download and print them from the Internet), coupons can save you plenty of money over time. But only use them for things you'd normally buy or wanted to try anyway.

Never shop when you're hungry. Have a snack before you hit the store.

In the store, walk around the perimeter and toward the back where the milk, fresh produce, and other basics are stocked so you don't have to go through all the tempting processed food aisles to get to them. End caps (small displays at the ends of aisles) are stocked with the most tempting nonnecessities, as are the areas near the checkout counters. Go past them to get in and get out—research shows the longer you stay, the more you'll spend.

Food on the go takes a heavy toll on the budget, so take your lunch to work and on outings to save a bundle. You'll save even more if you bring your coffee in a thermos.

Make sandwiches from peanut butter and jelly, sliced leftover pot roast or chicken, and other low-cost choices. (Don't use mayonnaise unless you can refrigerate lunch.) If you prefer a hot lunch, bring chili, spaghetti, goulash, or soup. Invest in good-quality, no-drip thermos containers for these favorites. If you like a little something extra, buy larger boxes of snack foods (try a generic brand to see if you can taste the difference) and repackage them in sandwich-sized zipper bags you can wash and reuse. In season, save by choosing fresh fruit and vegetable sticks (cut them yourself to save even more).

To beguile grandkids, cut deli boiled ham and cheese slices into circles, hearts, and stars using ordinary tin cookie cutters, then place the meat and cheese on round crackers and pop them into plastic sandwich bags or lunch boxes. The result: instant kiddie lunch treats at a lower cost.

Frugal Freezing and Luscious Leftovers

Freezing retains more vitamins than canning, but store-bought frozen foods are expensive. The solution: Buy extra of fresh foods your family likes when they're on sale and carefully freeze them yourself.

Invest in freezer-appropriate plastic bags and storage containers for leftovers. For extra protection, wrap meat in aluminum foil first. Label and date contents.

For "fast" food that's good for you and your budget, prepare two meals' worth of food every time you cook, and freeze one meal for the future.

Buy extra fresh fruit and vegetables in season and freeze for later. Lay berries or vegetable pieces on a tray to freeze individually before bagging so you can take out only what you need.

When strawberries, bananas, and other fresh fruits are just slightly oversoft, cut them up and add them to a blender with a little milk and sugar (or sweetener) for a healthful, delicious, low-cost smoothie.

"Enough is as good as a feast."
—JOHN HEYWOOD

Use meat and poultry leftovers in easy, semi-homemade dishes. Stir leftover chicken or pork morsels plus a few diced fresh carrots and green onion tops into chicken or pork ramen, and it's almost like carryout—but for pennies. Add hamburger or beef morsels and canned sliced mushrooms to cooked noodles along with a little cream of mushroom soup, and top with a dollop of sour cream for a budget stroganoff. Add ham bits to scrambled eggs or to baked beans to make them entrée-worthy.

Savvy Savings

Save the cookie crumbs left at the bottom of the cookie jar and the cereal crumbs left in the bottom of the box for frugal, great-tasting ice-cream toppings.

Plan a leftovers buffet night: Once a week, reheat your fridge leftovers (and any freezer leftovers approaching their prime), arrange them appetizingly, and serve them buffet-style. Let family members choose which they like best.

Don't buy sugar in packets: One packet of sugar costs about 500 times as much as the same amount of sugar bought in a five-pound bag.

Don't toss out leftover mashed potatoes. Freeze spoonfuls of them and store in ziplock freezer bags. You can use them later to make potato cakes or to thicken soups, stews, gravies, and sauces.

Speed baking time and save energy: Cut baking potatoes in half and bake them cut side down on a cookie sheet.

Don't buy bottled iced tea; brew tea from tea bags and let it cool on the counter. When it's room temperature, chill it in big pitchers. Optional: Add $\frac{1}{2}$ cup lemonade, punch, or orange juice for flavor.

Tap water in the United States is tested to be drinkable, so don't pay extra for bottled water. (In fact, tests have shown that some bottled waters have more germs than tap water, and many are just tap water or chemically purified well water.) If you dislike tap water's taste, install a purifier on your faucet, then pour water into pitchers and chill.

Save by making your own frozen microwave or toaster breakfasts. When you make pancakes, waffles, or French toast, make an extra batch and freeze individual portions in zippered plastic bags.

Don't toss hard brown sugar; just place the box in your microwave and heat it for 20 seconds. To save crystallized honey, place the jar in a pan filled with a little water, and gently heat on the stove.

For a fun, nutritious snack or dessert, buy grapes when they're on sale and freeze them.

To get twice the juice when you squeeze a lemon or other citrus fruit, microwave for 15 to 20 seconds before squeezing.

To make limp carrots, green peppers, or celery crisp again, soak in ice water for 30 minutes.

Use a metal colander as a vegetable steamer: Put vegetables in it, place the colander over a saucepan of boiling water, and cover.

When buying frozen fruit and vegetables, make sure you can feel the individual pieces through the bag. If the contents are one frozen lump, don't buy it; it has probably thawed and been refrozen.

To protect ice cream's taste and consistency once opened, cover it with waxed paper, plastic wrap, or aluminum foil before replacing the lid.

Don't buy expensive flavored sparkling water—make your own. Buy store-brand or generic club soda and add a small amount of juice or a few drops of fruit extract (such as strawberry or lemon) to make a low-calorie, inexpensive drink.

Mix that expensive coffee 50/50 with a lower-priced brand, and the rich flavors of your favorite brand will still come through.

When you make a pot of coffee, rinse a thermos coffee carafe with hot water, pour out, and refill with freshly made coffee. The coffee will stay hot without getting bitter, and you will save electricity.

To make low-cost frozen juice more appealing, mix it in the blender for a light and frothy treat.

Tenderize inexpensive cuts of meat so you can use them in recipes calling for higher-priced cuts: Soak the meat in a cup of vinegar overnight and rinse the vinegar off before cooking.

Marinate meats in a plastic bag instead of a pan and turn the bag over several times during the process. You'll use half the amount of marinade with the same results.

When milk starts to go sour, there's no need to throw it out. It's still safe to use in cooking. Use it right away in cake batter, cookie dough, or pancake batter. You can also use it in recipes calling for buttermilk.

Make your own inexpensive flavored coffee by adding cocoa, cinnamon, or almond or vanilla flavoring, or stir in a small chocolate mint candy.

In recipes, substitute cranberry or grape juice for red wine and apple juice for white wine.

Generics, House Brands, and Couponing

Try generic brands where appearance doesn't matter: toilet paper, plastic bags, aluminum foil, paper towels, and so forth. Generics are usually also fine for cooking.

For everything else, try store brands: Some are as good as nationally advertised brands and cost less—even when the advertised brand has a coupon.

Ask if the supermarket accepts another store's coupons or advertised specials. Many stores do but don't advertise it.

Don't buy something just because you have a coupon. Many coupons are for highly packaged convenience foods that are no bargain even with the coupon!

Voices from the Depression Era

"We lived on a farm, and I had a cousin just about my age who lived with us during the summer. On the farm we could always grow food and can or preserve it to eat in the winter, but there wasn't much variety and it wasn't fancy. I remember how thrilled we were when my uncle would come out on weekends to see my cousin. He brought us soft white bread from the store, salami and cheese, and sometimes hard candy—treats we never had otherwise! Nowadays people would pay more for the kind of whole-grain, homemade bread we ate every day, but like most kids, we wanted the soft, store-bought kind. To us, white bread was snack food!"   —Inger R.

If you are disappointed with a product, call the company's toll-free number (often listed on the back of the product package) and politely offer your feedback. Most companies will send a refund or replacement voucher.

For an inexpensive, low-calorie, high-protein food, buy eggs. They are one of the few foods that can be made into an entrée without adding any other ingredient. If you are not on a low-cholesterol diet, eggs can be used in a wide range of ways as a nutritional low-cost main course. Egg prices depend on their grade and size: Most supermarkets carry Grade AA and A; some also carry Grade B. All have the same nutritional value; the only difference is appearance.

To tell whether an egg is fresh, put it in water. A fresh egg will sink, but an old egg will float. Always buy eggs from a refrigerated egg case; those bought at room temperature from a farm or farmer's market will spoil much faster.

Don't store eggs, milk, cream cheese, or other perishables in the refrigerator door. Every time the door is opened they get a blast of warm air that spurs spoilage.

Healthy, Home-Grown Savings

Until after World War II, a small family vegetable garden was a common sight across the United States. Today, there's a move back toward locally grown, seasonal food to save money and energy and to eat healthfully. Even the White House has a small, organic garden today!

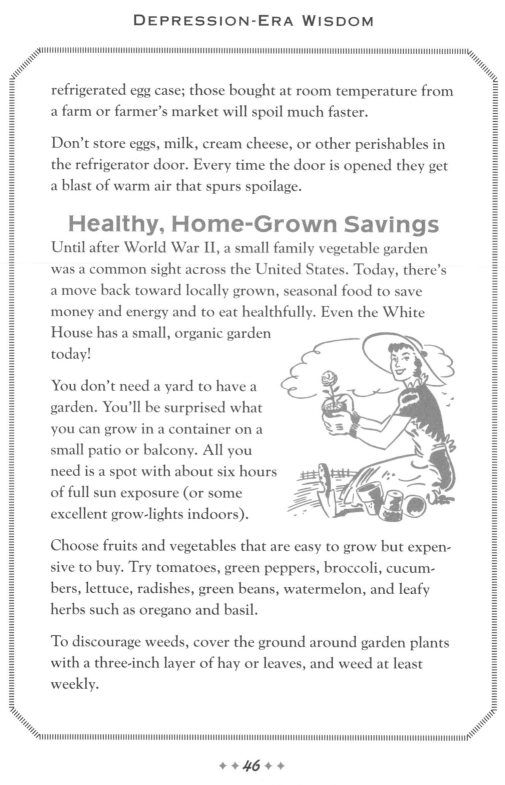

You don't need a yard to have a garden. You'll be surprised what you can grow in a container on a small patio or balcony. All you need is a spot with about six hours of full sun exposure (or some excellent grow-lights indoors).

Choose fruits and vegetables that are easy to grow but expensive to buy. Try tomatoes, green peppers, broccoli, cucumbers, lettuce, radishes, green beans, watermelon, and leafy herbs such as oregano and basil.

To discourage weeds, cover the ground around garden plants with a three-inch layer of hay or leaves, and weed at least weekly.

Shop garage sales and flea markets for quality used garden tools. All you need are a metal rake, a trowel, a hoe, and a pointed-tip shovel.

Ask your local park district how to make your own rain barrel or get one from their supply at nominal cost. Rain barrels enable you to use captured rain runoff to water your garden. It's free!

Savvy Savings

Make a low-cost drip irrigation system for your garden out of a leaky garden hose. Poke more holes in the hose with an ice pick or nail. Then lay the hose between the rows in your garden. Turn the water on low so that it will slowly drip out through the holes and soak into the ground.

For a low-cost lawn fertilizer, combine 1 cup Epsom salts and 1 cup household ammonia in a clean jar. To use, mix 2 tablespoons of the mixture with 2 gallons water in a watering can and sprinkle over 150 to 200 square feet of lawn.

Trade cuttings and seeds with neighbors and friends, and shop garage sales and flea markets for plants, pots, and garden tools.

Start seeds in cardboard egg cartons. You can plant carton and all!

Get a soil test from your local agricultural agent or cooperative so you'll know exactly what your soil lacks. The test is inexpensive (or possibly free!), and you won't waste money on useless additives.

Gifting on a Budget

During the Depression, folks did what they could and gave what they could. If you do fine needlework or woodcarving, a handmade gift could be ideal. If not, think outside the box. That applies to hospitality on a budget too!

Give heritage: Shop your china cabinet or attic for an heirloom treasure that will mean a lot, or trace your family tree online and share it with family members. Buy an inexpensive little notebook and write out favorite family recipes (you could also include this with a cookware gift for a family member's wedding).

Keep it real: If you don't have enough matching china for a large party, don't blow the budget on paper goods. Instead, alternate plates from various china patterns. (If you're serving buffet-style, stack the plates alternately on the buffet.) Alternate cups, glasses, flatware, and napkin patterns the same way. It will look charming, eclectic, and intentional!

Better than money is the gift of time and effort. Make (or have kids and teens make) a coupon book with offers to mow the lawn, babysit, clean out the garage, chauffeur, cook a special meal, and the like.

Search flea markets and garage sales for unique items to please someone with a special interest. For example, find an inexpensive, vintage cookbook or kitchen gadget for someone who loves to cook. Vintage buttons, tools, books, and sheet music all make nostalgic "thought of you" gifts.

*"He that burns logs that cost
nothing is twice warmed."*
—BENJAMIN FRANKLIN

Buy several small inexpensive items instead of one large gift, and package them together for impact. A kitchen package might include pot holders, dishcloths, and a cute salt-and-pepper set in an inexpensive wicker bread basket.

Give a photo album full of memorable pictures, and be sure to write names and dates on the back of each photo.

Record your voice reading fairy tales and send the recordings to grandchildren who live far away.

If you're crafty, create something; if you're not, shop craft shows and flea markets for one-of-a-kind creations without custom prices.

Voices from the Depression Era

"Getting food was a big deal for everybody. My dad was a precinct captain in Chicago, and I remember our whole dining room was filled with baskets of food, coupons to buy shoes, and other basics. Families in the precinct came to our house to pick up the donations they needed. My dad talked to them about local politics, of course, but the thing I remember is how much people appreciated the donations. They were really a lifeline." —Richard B.

CHAPTER 4

Tried-and-True Travel Tips

*I*n the 1930s, most trips were local. But that doesn't mean that the Depression era has nothing to offer when it comes to modern-day travel. Make the most of old-fashioned travel sense whenever possible. And when it's not possible to look to the past for savings tips, be sure to consider the modern-day wisdom we've compiled here.

Get Out of Town for Less

Roadhouses and local diners are in short supply these days, so stay at hotels that have a "free" breakfast. While quality and variety varies, you'll get enough of a choice to keep you until lunch.

Go back to the old-time schedule of making lunch your big meal instead of dinner. Most restaurants offer lunch menus that are very similar to dinner menus but at cheaper prices.

Bargain for hotel rates: Ask about special promotional rates, senior citizen discounts, a corporate rate, weekend rate, or group discounts for members of clubs or associations. Always review your lodging, car rental, or any other travel bills for errors.

*"Most families can afford to be
without the wonderful household
necessities no family can afford to be without."*
—ANONYMOUS

Call your insurance company before renting a car to find out if you are insured while driving a rental. If so, you can avoid paying for the expensive insurance offered through the rental car company.

Rather fly? Look for airfare bargains right after Christmas, Thanksgiving, or Easter. Plan ahead. To get most of the

Voices from the Depression Era

"When my brother and I were very small, my mother took us for a walk. My brother spotted someone walking down the street eating an ice-cream cone, and of course being a three-year-old, he wanted one too. He cried for my mother to buy him one. My mother tried to explain to him that she didn't have a penny to buy him an ice-cream cone. With tears in her eyes herself, she began to walk along the gutter in the street with us, in the hopes of finding a penny so that she could buy an ice-cream cone. She walked and searched for a long time and never did find a penny. Our parents survived the best they could on what very little they had to support their families. Even today, whenever I see a penny out in the street, I think of my mother walking and searching for such a long time just to find a penny to buy her children a little treat. I always stop and pick the penny up."   —Angela S.

bargain fares, you have to buy tickets 21 days in advance. If you can stay over Saturday night, it can drastically reduce your fare.

If you are flying to attend a funeral or family medical emergency, ask the airline about special reduced fares under their bereavement policy. Be ready to provide proof, such as a funeral notice or a letter from the doctor.

Save on a New Car

Cars were a luxury during the Depression, and next to housing, they're still the biggest single expense for most people. Luckily, today's shoppers have a lot more choices and a lot more ways to shop around.

Save time and money by pre-shopping for your car. Look at the price reference books and car buying guides at your local library and online to learn the dealer's cost plus the additional cost for each option. You can also check on the performance and maintenance records of different models. For objective ratings on new and used cars, check online or look to a consumer ratings group.

Then Versus Now

In 1930, the average cost of a new car was $640. By 1939, a car cost $700. In 1932, you could buy name-brand car tires for $3.69 each.

Once you find a car, factor in the annual cost of depreciation, repairs and maintenance, gas, and insurance. Consumer ratings groups offer statistics on depreciation, repairs, and maintenance costs on various popular models.

Remember: New cars start depreciating (losing value) the minute you drive them off the lot. After only four years, the average car is worth less than 40 percent of its selling price when new. Because new cars depreciate so much so quickly, the most frugal choice is to buy a relatively late-model used car.

Save on a Used Car

The ideal used car is one that is three years old or less, is in good condition both inside and out, and has been driven no more than 15,000 miles per year. The largest portion of depreciation will already have occurred on the car; any problems or defects will probably have worked themselves out and been repaired; and with reasonable care, the vehicle should still be reliable for at least another 50,000 miles.

When you find a used car you like, look it over carefully for signs of damage, excessive interior wear, missing or broken accessories, repainting, and other signs of trouble. Ask to see the maintenance and repair records,

Savvy Savings

Often, the best car prices are found at big-volume dealers, because they profit most from manufacturer incentives, and they may pass some of the savings on to you. If you have two dealerships close by, get a written estimate from one dealer and see if a competing dealership will beat the quoted price.

"Neither a borrower nor a lender be."
—WILLIAM SHAKESPEARE, *HAMLET*

if available. Test-drive the car on streets and highways and see how it handles at various speeds. Listen for unusual noises and turn on all accessories, including the air-conditioning and heater, to make sure they work. Finally, have your mechanic check out the car. If the seller refuses, move on. There are more cars than buyers out there in this economy.

To determine if the car you are looking at is priced fairly, use a guide from the library or an online resource such as the Kelley Blue Book (kbb.com). Guides like this one list the national average sale price, which may or may not apply in your particular area. Compare prices in your local newspaper's classified ads to get a feel for local prices.

Most used cars, even from a dealer, are sold expressly without a warranty. However, still-valid factory or extended warranties, or even service contracts, can sometimes be transferred to the new owner, so ask the dealer. You may be offered other insurance-type products, but they'll likely cancel out the

Savvy Savings

Make your own car windshield washer fluid by combining one cup rubbing alcohol, two tablespoons liquid detergent, and enough water to fill a gallon container. Mix and store the solution in a clean gallon jug. If desired, add a drop of blue food coloring. The alcohol will prevent the mixture from freezing.

savings you get from buying a used vehicle. The best assurance you have of a problem-free purchase is the reputation of your local dealer and the go-ahead from your own, trusted car mechanic who is not connected with the dealership. If you're buying from a non-dealer source, your mechanic's careful inspection becomes even more important. If you don't have a relationship with a mechanic, start asking around for names of people your friends and neighbors have found trustworthy.

Save on Financing

Whether you're buying new or used, save a lot on car loan interest: Finance for a shorter period of time or make a larger down payment. Contact several local financial institutions to find the lowest rate. A lower interest rate can save you hundreds over the life of the loan, so it pays to shop.

Save even more by paying cash. Look for a used car you like well enough to buy for the cash you can assemble, and skip the finance charges altogether. In this recession, you can negotiate a lower price and get more car for the money.

Consider selling your old car yourself: Clean it, tape a sign in the window, and run a small classified ad in the weekend edition of your local paper or online. If you'd rather trade in your car, look up the wholesale price. You can expect the dealer to pay you slightly less than this.

Save on Car Insurance

Comparison-shop your auto insurance every year, as rates can change drastically. Some companies will raise your rates

*"Beware of little expenses: a small
leak will sink a great ship."*
—BENJAMIN FRANKLIN

through the roof when you get a speeding ticket; others have "accident forgiveness" for a first incident. It's especially important to check rates when you add a driver, especially a teen driver, to your policy.

Ask each insurance company about discounts for cars with air bags, automatic seat belts, antitheft devices, and antilock brakes. Also ask whether they extend savings to drivers who are accident-free, are senior citizens, have taken a defensive driving course, are good students, or who drive fewer than a stipulated number of miles each year.

Increase your deductible for comprehensive and collision coverage, and you can cut your insurance rate considerably. Stash the saved money in a bank account so that you can easily come up with the deductible if you have to make a claim.

Save on Gas

Save wear and tear on your car as well as time and gas money: Combine errands into one trip, and call ahead to be sure the store has what you need before heading out.

Rev Up Gas Mileage

Many people buy high-octane gasoline because they think it will make their car perform better and run faster. This is just not the case. Only a few high-performance engines require premium

Then Versus Now

In 1930, a gallon of gas was 10 cents; in 1939, gas was still 10 cents a gallon.

gasoline (91 octane or higher) to avoid pinging. All other cars run on 87 octane, which is 10 cents to 30 cents a gallon cheaper. If you find that one brand knocks or pings, try a different brand before you spend the extra money on higher octane.

Drive 55. In addition to reducing the likelihood of costly accidents, the average car uses 17 percent less gasoline at 55 miles per hour than at 65 miles per hour.

If you belong to an auto club just for the towing benefit, check with your car insurance company to see if you can add towing coverage. In states that allow it, the costs are minimal—usually about $10 to $20 per year.

If you have more than one car, save 15 to 20 percent by insuring all of them with the same insurance company on the same policy.

AUTO INSURANCE

Never let your driver's license, car registration, or license tag expire: You'll end up paying the original fee plus an additional late fee that can be double or even triple the original amount due.

CHAPTER 5

Heat Up Energy Savings

*W*hen President Jimmy Carter told Americans to dial down the heat and put on a sweater in the 1970s, people laughed, but in the 1930s they knew better. During the Depression, keeping homes warm was a challenge, and keeping them cool was nearly impossible. What comfort people did achieve was mostly through a com-  bination of common-sense tactics based on physics. Today, half of U.S. home energy costs are in heating and cooling our houses, but you can use less energy—to the benefit of our planet—with some tried-and-true tricks.

Low-Tech Tips

Install white-backed draperies or shades, and on moderately warm summer days, close the draperies, shades, and windows on the south and west sides of the house. The white backing will reflect the sunlight and lower the temperature. Turn on fans to blow cooler air from the east and north sides through the house.

On sunny winter days, open draperies and shades (especially on the west and south sides of the house) to let in warming

"A small house is better than a large mortgage."
—ANONYMOUS

sunshine. Close them at night to help keep cold air out: Even the best windows are not walls!

Caulk and weather-strip all doors and windows. Look for cracks, both inside and outside, that allow winter chill or summer heat into the house, especially around window frames, air-conditioning units, vents, and wherever pipes enter the house.

Hot air rises, so in the winter, run a ceiling fan counter-clockwise (note that as you are looking up at the fan, it will actually appear to be moving clockwise) at the lowest speed to push the warmed air down. Run the fan clockwise (will appear to be moving counterclockwise) in the summer. Be sure the ceiling fan is no more than eight feet from the floor.

You may be losing more heat through your fireplace than a fire adds. Hot air rises, and your chimney is open to the sky, so it may actually be sucking expensive heat out of your home. Don't build a fire when it's bitter cold out; use it instead to take the chill out of a cold spring or fall evening.

To keep from losing furnace-warmed air all winter, close the damper on your fireplace as soon as the fire is completely out, and cover your fireplace with a glass or metal screen that fits the entire opening when you're not using it.

When you use air-conditioning, set your thermostat at 78 degrees Fahrenheit. It'll cost 20 percent less than if you set

it at 75 degrees and a whopping 40 percent less than at
72 degrees! Even set at a higher temperature, the air
conditioner will cut the humidity in your home and make it
more comfortable.

Don't place a lamp or TV near the air conditioner's thermostat. These appliances generate heat and can trick your air-
conditioning unit into running longer than necessary.

Turn off window air conditioners when you leave a room for
more than two hours. You can easily recool this small space
in a short time on your return. (Don't do this with central
air-conditioning: The cost to recool the whole house will
exceed short-term savings.)

Install a whole-house attic fan and cut down on the need for
air-conditioning. At low to moderate humidity levels, an attic

Voices from the Depression Era

"Even though my father was a licensed architect, he did
physical work in those days, such as painting walls, to
make ends meet. My mother used to give my twin sister
and me each a dime on Sunday afternoon so we could
go to the movies. Sometimes, though, painting jobs for
my dad were scarce, and she didn't have enough money
to give us each a dime, so she gave us each a nickel
instead. We were so disappointed at missing the movie
that it took us a while to take our nickels to the candy
store and make that our Sunday treat. We were lucky to
have that; a lot of kids didn't."   —Joyce N.

fan can make your house feel comfortable inside when it's 85 degrees outside!

Clean or replace the filter in your forced-air heating system and air conditioner every month they're in use.

When you use kitchen, bathroom, and other ventilating fans, turn them off as soon as they've done their job. In just one hour, these fans can blow away a houseful of warmed or cooled air.

The Lighter Side of Savings

Lights and household appliances account for a quarter of residential energy consumption, and there's plenty you can do to keep this use under control.

Switch to compact fluorescent lights (CFLs). They fit most incandescent lamp sockets and under many lampshades and provide the same quality of light. CFLs are three to four times as efficient as conventional lightbulbs and last ten times as long: An 18-watt compact fluorescent bulb provides the same amount of light as a 75-watt incandescent bulb. Initial purchase costs are higher for CFLs, but they pay for themselves in one year in electricity cost savings.

Appliance Energy Savings

Many utility companies offer much lower rates during off-peak hours, so use energy-intensive appliances such as dishwashers, washers, dryers, and electric ovens in the early morning or late evening.

To save big on a large appliance, ask to buy a floor model, but make sure parts, warranties, and service are still available.

When you buy a new appliance, look for a high Energy Efficiency Rating (EER). It may cost more initially, but an energy-efficient appliance will cost less to operate in the long run.

Refrigerators and freezers account for 15 percent of home energy costs, so next time, buy an energy-efficient model. Models made before 1986 are not energy-efficient.

Vacuum refrigerator coils to extend your refrigerator's useful life and to enable it to operate more effectively.

Test door seals to make sure they're not leaking and wasting energy: Close the refrigerator door over a dollar bill so it is half in and half out. If you can pull the dollar out easily, adjust the latch or replace the seal.

Don't store milk, cream cheese, or other highly perishable foods in the fridge door; because they're hit with warm air every time you open the fridge, they'll spoil faster.

Set a timer instead of opening the oven door to check on food. Every time you open the door, heat escapes, and you use more energy.

Then Versus Now

During the Great Depression, electric and gas appliances were as much a new thrill as the latest computer and iPod marvels are today. You could buy an electric toaster for $9.95, a gas refrigerator for $144.50, a washing machine for $33 to $59, or a gas stove priced from $20 to $70.

For about 87 percent of your cooking tasks, using the microwave oven can cut energy costs by at least 50 percent. In summer, ease your air-conditioning costs: Microwave so you don't heat up the kitchen.

On hot summer days, bake, roast, do laundry, and run the dishwasher early in the morning or late at night, as stoves, washers, dryers, and dishwashers add more heat to your rooms.

Good news: Washing dishes by hand typically uses more water than running the dishwasher, so use this convenience without guilt. To avoid waste, run the dishwasher only when it's full (but not overloaded) and run it on the right setting. Don't waste energy and water washing glassware on the pots-and-pans setting.

> ### Savvy Savings
>
> Think twice before you keep an old refrigerator around to provide extra chilling space. It may be costing you more than you think, especially if it's located in a garage where it's subjected to the extremes of hot and cold weather.

Water Savings

About 15 percent of home energy use goes to heating water, so don't waste it. Do as much household cleaning as possible with cold water, and repair leaky faucets promptly.

Install a water-saving aerator in your kitchen sink faucet and on all showerheads. They are inexpensive to buy—some utilities even provide them free. Aerators mix in air to let you reduce the actual amount of hot water used without reducing efficiency.

*"It is thrifty to prepare today for
the wants of tomorrow."*

—AESOP, *THE ANT AND THE GRASSHOPPER*

Use long baths as a therapeutic treat but take short showers for everyday bathing. It takes about 30 gallons of water to fill the average bathtub, but a shower with a flow of 3 gallons of water per minute uses only 15 gallons in 5 minutes. Assuming you use half hot and half cold water, you can save 5 gallons of hot water each time you take a shower instead of a bath.

Save "Loads" on Laundry

Keep both the lint screen in your dryer and the outside exhaust vent for the dryer clean. Check them regularly. A clogged exhaust lengthens drying time and wastes a lot of energy, and a clogged screen wastes energy and may cause house fires.

Hang clothes in the bathroom while you shower to steam out wrinkles and save time and energy otherwise spent ironing.

Wash one large load of laundry instead of two small or medium loads but never overload the machine.

Save water, detergent, and time when you need to presoak soiled clothes: Put them in the washing machine and let it fill, then let it stand before you run the normal cycle.

You'll pay a little more for a gas dryer than an electric one, but you'll spend less than half as much to operate it!